Clothes and Costumes

Written by
Nigel Nelson

Illustrated by
Tony De Saulles

Wayland

Books in the series

Clothes and Costumes   Landscapes

Conservation   Resources

Houses and Homes   Water

Journeys   Weather and Climate

First published in 1993 by
Wayland (Publishers) Ltd
61 Western Road, Hove
East Sussex, BN3 1JD, England

© Copyright 1993 Wayland (Publishers) Ltd

Series Editor: Mandy Suhr
Designer: Marilyn Clay

British Library Cataloguing in Publication Data

Nelson, Nigel
Clothes and Costumes. – (Starting Geography Series)
I. Title   II. Series
391

HARDBACK ISBN 0 7502 0332 3

PAPERBACK ISBN 0 7502 0802 3

Typeset in England by Dorchester Typesetting Group Ltd
Printed in Italy by Rotolito Lombarda, S.p.A., Milan

Contents

The words printed in **bold** are explained in the glossary.

Why clothes?

There are many reasons why we wear clothes. Clothes help to protect us from the weather.

If you live in a country with a cold **climate**, your clothes must keep you warm and dry. ▶

In a hot country, people wear clothes that will keep them cool. ▼

Some clothes are specially **designed** for the sort of work that people do.

This builder wears a hard hat to protect her head and overalls to keep her clean. ▶

We often wear special clothes on special occasions. These Scottish dancers are wearing **kilts**. What kind of special clothes do you wear?

The first clothes

Unlike most animals, people do not have much hair or fur to keep them warm. Some of the first people lived in places with very cold climates. They made clothes to keep them warm by sewing together animal **hide** or fur.

These **Inuit** children in Canada are wearing clothes made from **Caribou** hide. The thick fur helps to keep them warm.

The first people who lived where the climate was warmer found out how to **weave** animal and plant **fibres**, like wool, cotton and grass. Some clothes were even made from the bark of trees.

This girl from Hawaii is wearing **traditional** style clothes made from grasses, palm leaves, flowers and feathers. ▶

Activity

Make a collage picture using natural things like leaves, flower petals and grasses. Make sure you ask an adult before you pick any flowers.

Get weaving!

Many clothes today are made from **woven** cloth. The wool from animals such as sheep, or the **llama** in this picture, is used to make warm, woolly clothes. ▲

◄ Some plant fibres are used to make cooler clothes, such as this **cotton** grown in the USA.

To make woven cloth, the fibres or wool are **spun** together to make thread. ▶
The thread is **dyed** bright colours and then woven into cloth on a **loom**.

This colourful cloth is being made by hand in Guatemala. But most fabric these days is made on large machine looms in huge factories.

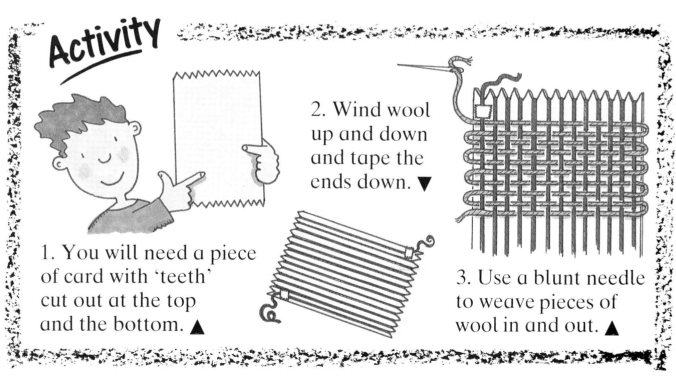

Activity

1. You will need a piece of card with 'teeth' cut out at the top and the bottom. ▲

2. Wind wool up and down and tape the ends down. ▼

3. Use a blunt needle to weave pieces of wool in and out. ▲

Clothes for sale

Many clothes today are made in factories like this. ▶

The clothes are sold to people in shops and markets. Clothes made in one country are often sold to people living in another country.

Clothes are **transported** from one country to another by ship or aeroplane.

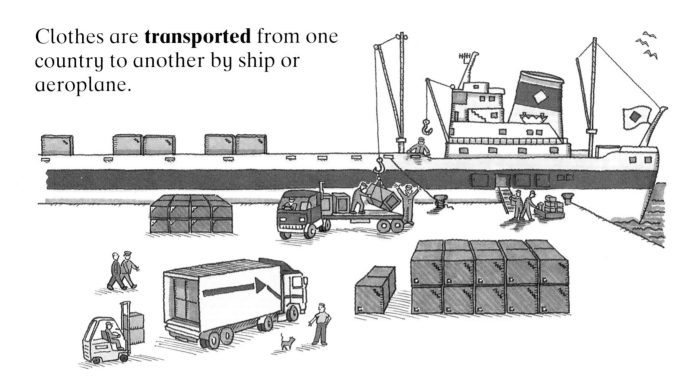

The shops you buy your clothes from probably sell clothes made in many different countries.

Look at the labels in your clothes. Can you find out where they have been made? Find the countries on a globe or map of the world.

It's a tradition

People from different places often have their own way of dressing. This may be a **traditional costume**. These children are wearing traditional costumes from Portugal. ▲

Traditional costumes are passed down from parents to their children. Sometimes they are worn for special occasions. The clothes may look quite different to clothes worn in other places.

Traditional costumes were often designed to suit different kinds of weather. These Lapp people are wearing traditional clothes that protect them from the cold climate that they live in. ▶

The traditional costume of a whole country is called a **national costume**. These children are dressed in the national costume of Sweden.

Going east

The traditional costume of Japan is the **kimono**. This is a loose robe wrapped over in front and tied with a **sash**. Most are made from brightly coloured **silk**. It was the Chinese people who discovered how to make silk hundreds of years ago.

Silk is made from the fibres that silkworms spin around their bodies to make a **cocoon**. ▲

The fibres are spun together to make thread. Then they are dyed and woven into silk cloth. ▲

Thailand is also famous for its silk. These Thai costumes are very expensive and are only worn on special occasions. ▼

Clothes and religion

The religion of a country or a group of people often affects the sort of clothes they wear. The **Native Americans** of Canada and the USA believe in the magic powers of the animal skins, feathers and claws that they wear for special celebrations.

Some religions say that a woman should cover her head and face. This woman from Morocco is wearing a veil and shawl.

These Christian children in the Seychelles are dressed in white clothes to celebrate a special day at their church.

Special days

People everywhere have different days which are important to them. They often wear special clothes on such special days. Sometimes people celebrate an important event on the same day every year. Your birthday is probably your most important day. You might dress up in your best clothes and have a party.

Other special events, like weddings, may take place once. This couple are dressed in special wedding clothes.

Carnival time

Many types of Carnival take place all over the world. It is a happy time when people stop work and go out into the streets to dance, sing and enjoy themselves. These children are dressed in brightly coloured Carnival costumes at the Notting Hill Carnival in London, England.

Activity

Design your own Carnival costume.

Probably the biggest Carnival is in Rio de Janeiro in Brazil. Carnival is a time when both rich and poor people can be equal. Many poor Brazilians save up all year to pay for their fantastic costumes.

Uniforms

People wear uniforms in all sorts of jobs throughout the world.

Uniforms are designed to suit the job for which they are worn. This woman is a police officer in Canada. Her uniform helps people to recognize her quickly.

These soldiers in Britain belong to a special group called the Horse Guards. They guard the Queen's palace in London.

A uniform can show that you belong to a special group. Sports teams wear a kind of uniform.

All the members of a team have a similar outfit in their team colours.

Many children wear a school uniform. This shows which school they go to. These children go to school in Kenya.

Accessories

Accessories, like bags, gloves, scarves and belts, can be useful as well as decorative. These children are wearing colourful hats to keep their heads warm. ▲

Jewellery is worn by people all over the world. Sometimes it is worn in traditional ways. This girl from Pakistan is wearing a gold hair decoration and nose ring. ▶

◄ This African jewellery is made from hundreds of tiny beads.

Painting parts of the body is a tradition in many countries. This Indian girl has painted patterns on her hands with a dye called **henna**. ▼

Activity

Make your own jewellery. Make a bracelet or necklace by threading beads, buttons or pieces of plastic straw onto a length of thin string or wool.

Choose your shoes

Shoes protect our feet from being hurt on the rough ground. They also help to keep our feet warm. The Inuit people who live in the freezing **Arctic** still use animal furs to make warm boots. ▶

In warm weather, people often wear sandals. Sandals allow a lot of air to get to your feet. This keeps them cool. ▼

People wear special shoes for special purposes. Training shoes were first made for playing sport. Now many people wear them as everyday shoes, like these boys in New York, USA.

How many different kinds of shoes can you think of? What are they used for?

What's the fashion?

These days fashions change much more quickly than they did in the past. As people travel from one country to another, they spread new ideas about clothes and styles of dress.

In Africa you will find people wearing European clothes as well as their own traditional clothes. ▶

In the same way, people from European countries like to wear traditional African printed cotton clothes. ▼

Denim jeans were first made in the USA over a hundred years ago. They were made to be hard-wearing trousers for working men. Now millions of them are worn all around the world. ▲

Clothes are now being made from many new materials like plastic, metal and even paper!
What do you think clothes will look like in the future? ▶

Glossary

Arctic The cold, icy areas around the North Pole.

Caribou A type of deer.

Climate A pattern of weather.

Cocoon A covering which protects an insect grub while it is changing into an adult insect.

Cotton A plant that produces soft white fibres around its seeds. These fibres are used to make cotton material.

Designed Made in a special way.

Dyed Stained a certain colour.

Fibres Thin strings or strands.

Henna An orange dye made from the leaves of the henna plant.

Hide An animal's skin.

Inuit A group of people who live along the Arctic coasts of North America and Greenland.

Kimono A long loose robe worn in Japan.

Kilt A knee-length pleated skirt made from tartan fabric worn traditionally in Scotland.

Llama An animal from South America. It has soft woolly hair.

Loom A machine that is used to weave cloth.

National costume A costume that is traditionally worn in one country.

Native Americans The first people to live in America, who lived there before Europeans.

Sash A long strip of cloth tied round the waist like a belt.

Silk A rich, shiny material made from the fibres spun by silkworms.

Spun Pulled out and twisted together to make thread.

Traditional Something that has stayed the same for many years or been handed down through a family.

Traditional costume A type of dress that has stayed the same for many years.

Transported Moved from one place to another.

Weave A way of making cloth by passing lengths of thread in and out of each other.

Woven Made by weaving.

Finding out more

Books to Read
From Cotton to T-shirt by Nicola Baxter (Simon and Schuster, 1992)
My Book About Clothes by Wayne Jackman (Wayland, 1991)
New Shoes by Kate Petty (A&C Black, 1992)
Our Clothes (series) (Wayland, 1990)
People and Customs (series) (Macmillan, 1979)

Useful Addresses
The Horniman Museum
London Road
London SE23

The Commonwealth Institute
Kensington High Street
London W8

The Victoria and Albert Museum
Cromwell Road
London W8

Museum of Mankind
6 Burlington Gardens
London W1X 2EX

British Wool Marketing Board
Oak Mills
Station Road, Clayton
Bradford, W. Yorks.

Textile Institute
10 Blackfriars Street
Manchester, M3 5DR

Picture acknowledgements
B&C Alexander 4 (above), 6, 13 (below left), 16 (right), 22 (below), 26 (above); J. Allan Cash Ltd. 5 (below), 23 (above), 24 (above); Cephas 9; Chapel Studios 5 (above), 14, 19, 22 (above); Bruce Coleman 7, 15 (above left); Eye Ubiquitous 12, 15 (above right), 20, 28 (below); Tony Morrison South American Pictures 8 (above), 9 (left); Christine Osbourne Pictures 22, 23 (below), 24 (below), 25 (right); Panos Pictures 10 (above), 27 (below); Photri Inc. 13 (right), 15 (below), 21; Tony Stone Worldwide 18, 26 (below), 42; Tropix 28 (above); Zefa COVER, 4 (below), 8 (below), 10 (below), 16 (left), 25 (left), 27 (above).

Index